DEEPER INTO THE HEART OF GOD

A 40 Day Guided Journal

By Perry-May Britton

© Perry-May

INTRODUCTION

Welcome to this 40 day journey going deeper into the heart of God. The purpose of this journal is to help you get to know Father God, understand His character and find your place in the story.

Each day you will have a short **bible reading,** some ideas for your **journal,** an **action** and then an encouragement to **pray**. You will need at least five minutes each day, a modern bible and something to write with. You could do this with your family or a group of friends.

The readings are intended to highlight one or two small points but if you have time it is always good to read around the verse, discover the context in which it was written and invest in your knowledge of the bible.

You do not have to complete this in 40 days, you could take a week over each theme. There is a cutout page designed for you to take with you as a bookmark and to help you read, journal and connect well with God.

There are four sections:
- Preparing for the journey
- The Character of God
- Our Story in God's Story
- Our Response

At the back of the journal is a prayer. You can pray this at any time on your journey.

I hope this is a life changing adventure and that you fall in love with God on the way. You are unique and special and He is excited to spend time with you in this way.

God bless your journey. Peny-May

ABOUT THE AUTHOR

This journal was written and illustrated by Perry-May Britton. She is married to Mike and mum to Joshua and they live in a little cottage in Rural England. They love people, entertaining and living simply. They have one small dog and a large flock of cheeky chickens.

Perry-May knows and loves the Lord and takes great delight in helping others grow deeper in their relationship with the Lord.

You can find out more on www.perry-may.com

✂...CUT THIS PAGE OUT AND TAKE IT WITH YOU EACH DAY

EACH DAY:

Read the passage: You could read it out aloud several times slowly or you could try reading it in different versions of the bible. If you have time, read the whole chapter or find out the context in which it is written. Good questions to ask yourself as you read are: What does this say? What does it mean? And How does it apply to me?

Journal: It is entirely up to you what you write. You can follow the suggestion or simply write down what you feel the Lord is speaking to you about. I sometimes like to write down the verses that jump out at me or just doodle and enjoy the time being with the Lord!

Action: I love doing small prophetic acts because they help me ground my faith journey, they show God that I really mean business and create helpful memories that link to truth.

Pray: I don't want to dictate how you should use your prayer time but here are some ideas:

1 Pray through the Lord's Prayer slowly and deliberately:

   Our Father in heaven, hallowed be your name
   your kingdom come, your will be done,
   on earth as in heaven.
   Give us today our daily bread.
   Forgive us our sins as we forgive those
   who sin against us.
   Lead us not into temptation but
   deliver us from evil.
   For the kingdom, the power, and
   the glory are yours
   Now and for ever. Amen.

2 Repeat what is called The Jesus Prayer several times: "Lord Jesus Christ, Son of God, have mercy on me, a sinner." Take this prayer with you into your day.

3 You could write out your prayers.

4 Make a list of people and situations you are praying for so you can turn to it regularly. It's fun to have a note especially so that you can go back over it and make notes of answered prayer.

5 Take God with you on a prayer walk.

6 Hold something from nature as you pray, a pebble, a smooth piece of wood, an acorn or a waxy leaf. It's a lovely way of grounding yourself within God's creation.

It doesn't matter how you pray, all that matters is that you do!

PART ONE
Preparing for the journey

DAY ONE: ARE YOU THIRSTY?

READ: Isaiah 55:1-3

JOURNAL IDEA: Are you thirsty for the Lord? What areas of your life feel dry? Write a prayer committing to go on this journey with God.

ACTION: Pour yourself a long cool glass of water. Drink it slowly. Enjoy it and imagine God is quenching all your spiritual thirst.

AND PRAY...

DAY TWO: SEEK FIRST HIS KINGDOM

READ: Matthew 6:25-34

JOURNAL IDEA: Write down all the things you are worried about and give them to God in prayer. Decide to leave them behind as you go on this adventure. Then commit to seeking Him first.

Leave your sack of worries at His feet. ♡

ACTION: Try making a prayer box. Find a pretty box, write all your prayers and worries on small bits of paper (with the date next to them). As you put them in, pray over them and give them to God. You can add to it any time. Every now and again go through it and see if anything has been answered... put those in another box called 'answered prayer'.

AND PRAY...

DAY THREE: THE HEAVENS DECLARE THE GLORY OF GOD

READ: Psalm 19:1-6

JOURNAL IDEA: If you are struggling to find God, start with nature... write about a time when you saw something beautiful in nature - a bird, an animal, a tree...

ACTION: Make time to watch a sunset or a sunrise this week.

AND PRAY...

You could do a little doodle here!

PART TWO
The Character of God

DAY FOUR: HE WANTS TO BE FOUND

READ: Isaiah 55:6 and Deuteronomy 4:29

JOURNAL IDEA: What does it feel like to know that God actually wants you to find Him? How do you think you could pursue Him?

God hiding... He wants you to find Him.

ACTION: Play (or imagine playing) hide and seek with a small child! Think about how it works... now imagine you are the child playing hide and seek with God.

AND PRAY...

DAY FIVE: HE FORGIVES YOU FREELY

READ: Psalm 103:1-5

JOURNAL IDEA: Re-write this Psalm and personalise it, put your name in it, say 'me' instead of you… make it your own.

Watch your sin and shame go up in flames! ♥

ACTION: Write down the things you are ashamed of on a piece of paper. If you can do it safely, burn the page and give your shame to God. He has purged these sins and can't remember them any more.

AND PRAY…

DAY SIX: HE IS COMPASSIONATE & MERCIFUL

READ: Psalm 86:15-16

JOURNAL IDEA: Consider how God's compassion and mercy intertwine with your heart. How teachable do you think you are?

He wraps your heart with compassion & mercy.

MERCY & COM

ACTION: Find a worship song about His compassion and mercy and lie on the floor listening to it.

AND PRAY...

DAY SEVEN: HE IS YOUR FORTRESS

READ: 2 Samuel 22:1-7

JOURNAL IDEA: Remember a time you have been rescued from a situation and write about it and how it made you feel.

ACTION: Draw a picture of yourself inside God's safe place.

AND PRAY...

DAY EIGHT: HE IS YOUR RESCUER

READ: 2 Samuel 22:17-20

JOURNAL IDEA: Write about letting God rescue you and what it might mean.

ACTION: Go for a walk where you can see the horizon, a spacious place. Take God with you.

AND PRAY...

DAY NINE: HE IS YOUR REFUGE AND STRENGTH

READ: Psalm 46

JOURNAL IDEA: Write about your fears to God and then let him melt them away.

Let your fears melt away. ♡

ACTION: Pop an ice cube on a pretty plate. Sit and watch it melt… 'Be still, and know that I am God;…' v10.

AND PRAY...

DAY TEN: HE IS YOUR PROTECTOR

READ: Psalm 91:9-13

JOURNAL IDEA: How do you feel about the fact that God sends His angels to guard you? Are you able to say 'The Lord is my refuge'?

There are angels all around you.

ACTION: Get a duvet or a warm blanket and wrap it around you. Imagine it is God is giving you a hug and making you feel secure.

AND PRAY...

DAY ELEVEN: HE IS ACCEPTING

READ: Romans 15:7-13

JOURNAL IDEA: Write about what it means for God to accept you. What are the implications of this for you?

ACTION: Think about someone you could encourage today - then do it (it doesn't have to be face to face).

AND PRAY...

DAY TWELVE: HE IS KIND

READ: Jeremiah 31:3-6

JOURNAL IDEA: Write down your personal response to God's unfailing kindness / everlasting love.

Let kindness pop out of you!

ACTION: Sometimes it's those closest to us, family members or best friends that we take for granted. Do an act of kindness for someone near you.

AND PRAY...

DAY THIRTEEN: HE IS TENDER HEARTED

READ: Luke 1:67-80

JOURNAL IDEA: Write all the words that describe God in this passage. Then focus on the last few verses and think how you could grow strong in spirit like John.

ACTION: Make or draw a heart that represents the Lord's heart. Put it somewhere as a little reminder each day (next to your mirror, at the front door, above the loo roll!)

AND PRAY...

DAY FOURTEEN: HE WALKS WITH YOU

READ: Hosea 11:1-4

JOURNAL IDEA: You are Israel and God is your father – write down the times you know he has cared for you or walked with you. It's so good to remember his faithfulness.

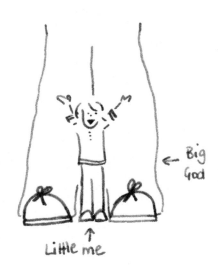

ACTION: Go for another walk with God. As you walk, ask him for guidance over the rough terrain in your life.

AND PRAY...

DAY FIFTEEN: HE IS FAITHFUL

READ: Hebrews 13:1-6

JOURNAL IDEA: Do a search through the bible and find out how many places God promises to never leave you or forsake you.

God's promise to you.

ACTION: Think of a practical way you can respond to these verses: hospitality? Prayer? writing letters? Visiting?

AND PRAY...

DAY SIXTEEN: HE IS COMMITTED TO YOUR FLOURISHING

READ: Romans 8:28-32

JOURNAL IDEA: This is such a rich passage! Write some of it out but make it personal eg 'I know that God works for my good because I love him….'

Me flourishing!

ACTION: Memorise as much of this chapter as you can!

AND PRAY…

DAY SEVENTEEN:
HE REJOICES OVER YOU WITH SINGING

READ: Zephaniah 3:17

JOURNAL IDEA: Write a worship song or a poem to God.

ACTION: Try to have worship music playing in the background for a whole day.

AND PRAY...

DAY EIGHTEEN: HE IS PATIENT

READ: 2 Peter 3:8-9

JOURNAL IDEA: Write about something you are waiting for. Then commit it to the Lord and ask Him to help you see His perspective.

ACTION: Climb a hill or a tree or go to the top of a building… somewhere where you can look down. Ask the Lord to help you see with His eyes.

AND PRAY…

DAY NINETEEN: HE IS APPROACHABLE

READ: Hebrews 4:14-16

JOURNAL IDEA: Write down anything that hinders you from approaching God. Then thank Him that Jesus has made a way.

ACTION: Find a lovely pebble and hold it. God loves to connect with us through the simple things.

AND PRAY...

DAY TWENTY: HE IS THE GOOD SHEPHERD

READ: John 10:7-15

JOURNAL IDEA: We are half-way through our 40 days. It's a good day to take stock and ask yourself 'am I following the good shepherd?' and if not, you might like to decide to do so. Write a prayer of commitment to following Him.

"I'm sticking close to the good shepherd."

ACTION: Pray through the prayer at the back of this journal and then tell someone who would love to hear this news.

AND PRAY...

DAY TWENTY-ONE: HE IS LOVE

READ: 1 John 4:13-21

JOURNAL IDEA: Write a prayer inviting the Holy Spirit to fill you afresh with his Love.

God showering the Holy Spirit on you!

ACTION: Get a glass of water and some salt. Imagine the glass of water is God's love and the salt is your fears… using a spoon put your fears (some salt) into the water, stir it and watch as God's love dissolves your fears. Perfect love drives out fear.

AND PRAY…

Another little doodle page!

PART THREE
Our Story in God's Story

DAY TWENTY-TWO:
YOU ARE CREATED IN HIS IMAGE

READ: Genesis 1:27-31

JOURNAL IDEA: When God looks at you he sees that it is VERY GOOD - write about how that makes you feel.

ACTION: Draw yourself (it can be a stick figure) and draw or write around yourself all the characteristics you have that make you like God eg. I am kind, I am creative…

AND PRAY…

DAY TWENTY-THREE: YOU ARE KNOWN

READ: Psalm 139:1-6

JOURNAL IDEA: Write out these verses in full. Then write a declaration about how glad you are that God knows you so completely.

ACTION: Take some time to sit with these words. What does it mean to be this well-known? What difference does it make to your life? What can you do knowing you are KNOWN and LOVED completely?

AND PRAY...

DAY TWENTY-FOUR:
YOU ARE HIS NEW CREATION

READ: 2 Corinthians 5:17-21

JOURNAL IDEA: Write about what it means to be a new creation through what Christ has done.

Yummy! I made this.

ACTION: Make something new: bake a cake, write a poem, write a story, use clay… anything. Make something new and enjoy it!

AND PRAY...

DAY TWENTY-FIVE: YOU ARE HIS HEIR

READ: Romans 8:14-17

JOURNAL IDEA: What does it mean to be an heir? How does it feel to be the child of the King?

Put on your crown
Your Dad is THE KING!

ACTION: Make yourself a crown and wear it!

AND PRAY...

DAY TWENTY-SIX:
YOU CAN HEAR HIS VOICE

READ: John 10:3-5

JOURNAL IDEA: List ways that you have heard God in the past and ask him to speak to you today.

ACTION: Do some research into the ways God speaks and eagerly pursue hearing him.

AND PRAY...

DAY TWENTY-SEVEN:
YOU ARE GENTLY LED

READ: Isaiah 40:11

JOURNAL IDEA: The Good Shepherd tends, gathers and carries you close to his heart… write how you can be more 'sheep-like'.

ACTION: Find a friend or family member you trust, shut your eyes and ask them to guide you somewhere. As you do it, imagine you are saying to God 'yes, I will follow you'…

AND PRAY...

DAY TWENTY-EIGHT:
YOU RECEIVE STRENGTH FROM HIM

READ: Isaiah 40:28-31

JOURNAL IDEA: What does it mean to you to put your hope in the Lord?

ACTION: Read through this whole chapter. It is so rich and full and speaks of so much that you have already studied.

AND PRAY...

DAY TWENTY-NINE:
YOU ARE ALLOWED TO DREAM

READ: Psalm 126

JOURNAL IDEA: It is very hard for a slave to dream about his future, but an heir can dream. write your dreams down and commit them to God.

ACTION: Plant something in your garden or a small pot on the windowsill… then tend to it and imagine it is your dreams.

AND PRAY…

DAY THIRTY:
YOU ARE TAKEN TO THE BANQUET

READ: Song of Songs 2:4-6

JOURNAL IDEA: What does it mean to have a banner over you called 'LOVE'?

ACTION: Prepare a 'banquet' or special meal for someone you love.

AND PRAY...

DAY THIRTY-ONE: YOU NEED NOT FEAR

READ: Isaiah 43:1-3

JOURNAL IDEA: Write about what it is like to be known by name.

ACTION: Research all the times it says 'Do not fear' in the bible... apparently there is one for every day of the year!

AND PRAY...

DAY THIRTY-TWO: GOD HAS GOOD PLANS FOR YOU

READ: Jeremiah 29:11-14

JOURNAL IDEA: What is your part in this deal with God? How can you seek him with all your heart?

ACTION: Do a prophetic act... stand and jump into something, a field, a room, onto a carpet - as you do it declare that you are jumping into God's plans for your life.

AND PRAY...

Doodle page.

PART FOUR
Our Response

DAY THIRTY-THREE:
COMMIT YOUR WAY TO THE LORD

READ: Psalm 37:3-7

JOURNAL IDEA: These verses give some very clear instructions. Write down how you can put them into practice.

ACTION: Pray the prayer at the back of this book if you are able to, if you have done it before, it is sometimes good to do it again, to remind yourself what you believe.

AND PRAY…

DAY THIRTY-FOUR: REPENT AND BE FILLED WITH THE HOLY SPIRIT

READ: Acts 2: 38-39

JOURNAL IDEA: Write an invitation to the Holy Spirit to come and fill you up.

God's Holy Spirit descended on Jesus like a dove.

ACTION: Kneel while you pray.

AND PRAY...

DAY THIRTY-FIVE: THANK HIM

READ: Psalm 9:1-2

JOURNAL IDEA: Write a thank you letter to God.

ACTION: Write a list or start a new book where you can write all the things you are thankful for. When you are having a bad day turn to it and remember the Lord's goodness.

AND PRAY...

DAY THIRTY-SIX: WORSHIP HIM

READ: Psalm 33: 1-9

JOURNAL IDEA: Write your own Psalm of worship to the Lord.

Worship with your whole being.

ACTION: Put on some loud worship music, sing and dance around the room.

AND PRAY...

DAY THIRTY-SEVEN: GIVE GENEROUSLY

READ: 2 Corinthians 9:6-8

JOURNAL IDEA: Write about the best gift you have ever received and its impact on you.

Giving generously makes you feel good inside.

ACTION: Give away some money, some thing or some of your time. God loves a cheerful giver!

AND PRAY...

DAY THIRTY-EIGHT: LOVE OTHERS

READ: Matthew 22:37-40

JOURNAL IDEA: Who do you think Jesus means is your neighbour? Write about how the Lord is telling you to love your neighbour.

For you!

ACTION: Do something unexpected and kind for someone else.

AND PRAY...

DAY THIRTY-NINE: TELL OTHERS

READ: Matthew 28:16-20

JOURNAL IDEA: This is called the great commission... what does it mean to 'make disciples' and how can you do your part?

ACTION: Ask God to show you someone you could tell about Jesus... and then tell them!

AND PRAY...

DAY FORTY: CHOOSE JOY

READ: Isaiah 55:12-13

JOURNAL IDEA: Let's end where we started with Isaiah 55. Some days we need to choose joy. Draw yourself full of joy!

ACTION: Thank the Lord for the adventure you have been on these last 40 days and look back, highlighting the strong themes that God has used to speak to you.

AND PRAY, AND KEEP ON PRAYING...

Prayer of Commitment

Dear God, I am sorry for the things I have done, said or thought that have not pleased you (this bit is called repentance).

Thank you that you died on a cross for me so that I can have a relationship with you.

Please come into my life, fill me with your Holy Spirit and help me to walk out the rest of my days with you.

Thank you Lord, Amen.

I am so delighted you have prayed this prayer. **Now go and tell someone!**

Thank you for coming on this journey with me. Don't stop reading your bible, walking with Jesus, loving your Father or serving Him. Remember, He has GREAT plans for you… now it's time to step into them.

God bless you.

Perry-May

Printed in Great Britain
by Amazon